Bob et Ben à Boulogne

Voici Bob et Ben à la gare.

Voici Bob et Ben dans le train.

C'est Folkestone. Passeports!

Voici Bob et Ben sur le bateau.

5

ACTIVITES BIBLIOBUS

A Choose the correct words to finish each of these sentences.

1. Bob and Ben arrive in
   (a) Boulogne.
   (b) Paris.
   (c) the police station.

2. The ice-creams cost
   (a) three francs.
   (b) four francs.
   (c) five francs.

3. Ben asks the lady in the street the way to
   (a) the station.
   (b) the ice-cream seller.
   (c) the police station.

4. Ben says he is
   (a) ten.
   (b) eleven.
   (c) twelve.

5. The first question the policeman asks is
   (a) Ben's name.
   (b) Ben's address.
   (c) Ben's age.

B The names of all these things begin with the same letter — except one! Which one?

On joue au football

Voici Albert.

Il arrive au collège.

CES JEANNE D'ARC

Bonjour, la classe. Voici Albert.

Regarde !

Qui est-ce ?

C'est le professeur. Il s'appelle monsieur Bardot.

C'est la classe.

C'est Bernard.
C'est le chef.

C'est Julie.

C'est Sébastien.

C'est Alain.

C'est Raymond.

C'est le professeur de sport.
Il s'appelle monsieur Laballe.

Bernard est furieux.

ACTIVITES BIBLIOBUS

A The answer to each of these questions is the name of someone in the story. Who is it?

1. Qui arrive au collège?

2. Qui est le chef?

3. Qui est le professeur de sport?

4. Qui est furieux?

5. Qui est le champion?

B Can you find the two long words caught in the net? Start at the F each time. Move one square at a time up, down or across. (Both the words mean "great!".)

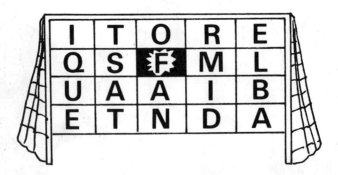